style
to go

Kitchens

style
to go

Kitchens

JOSH GARSKOF

The Taunton Press

The Taunton Press, Inc., 63 South Main Street,
PO Box 5506, Newtown, CT 06470-5506
e-mail: tp@taunton.com

Jacket/Cover design: Allison Wilkes
Interior design: Kimberly Adis, Allison Wilkes
Layout: Amy Russo

Library of Congress Cataloging-in-Publication Data
Garskof, Josh.
  Style to go-- kitchens / Josh Garskof.
     p. cm.
  ISBN-13: 978-1-56158-933-3
  ISBN-10: 1-56158-933-0
  1. Kitchens. 2. Interior decoration. I. Title. II. Title: Style
to go. III. Title: Kitchens.

NK2117.K5G37 2007
747.7'97--dc22

                                    2006020155

Printed in China
10 9 8 7 6 5 4 3 2 1

contents

design &
style

Modern materials—aluminum, glass, and concrete—bring a contemporary flair to a time-honored kitchen feature: a space-saving breakfast nook.

A raised floor, ceiling-hung shelf, and thick column help to define the boundaries of a kitchen located within a great room.

Want the effect of an island without the cost?

Add a table that can double as work surface and eating area.

This new kitchen has a 19th-century farmhouse feel thanks to an apron sink, furniture-style cabinet feet, mosaic floor tile, bin pull cabinet hardware, and a gooseneck faucet.

Chrome bin pulls, glass pendant lights over the island, and the brackets holding up the buffet fit perfectly in a Craftsman-style bungalow.

If the view out your kitchen window is anything but beautiful, consider trading the window for glass block, which lets in light but hides unsightly scenery.

With the variety of stock windows now available, you're sure to find units that fit the architecture of your home and let in just the right amount of light.

A unique two-tone cabinet paint job and an island created by two antique farm tables give this kitchen a period look.

The color black—on the countertops, ceiling reveals, and toe kicks—helps to unify the diverse components in this contemporary kitchen.

For a kitchen made up of pale neutral colors, visual interest comes from patterns of squares in the backsplash, flooring, and window treatment.

Who says an up-to-date kitchen has to cost a fortune? Stock cabinets—in both natural wood and metal and glass—and fire slate countertops cost a fraction of custom woodwork and granite.

Above: V-groove cabinet backs and rustic wood finishes create a Western ambiance.

Right: Mixing cabinet finishes can create an unfitted look but not here. The freestanding hutch and island are natural choices for bold color since their presence commands attention. White porcelin knobs tie everything together.

The contrasting textures
of beadboard cabinets,
diamond print wallpaper,
checked stools, and speckled
stone countertops give this
wheat-colored kitchen visual
appeal.

Left Beadboard paneling, box beams, and long pendant lights help to lower the expansive feel of a 10-ft.-high ceiling in this remodeled Victorian home.

A wall of colorful glass mosaic tiles turns an eating nook into the focal point of the kitchen.

If your kitchen
is part of a
larger great room,
repeat
some of the
colors
throughout the whole
space to provide
visual connection.

A medley of purples,
blues, greens, and oranges
gives this kitchen its
colorful character. Open
shelves help to alleviate a
closed-in feeling.

Colorful tiles, like this backsplash of fruits and vegetables, make a bold statement in a subdued kitchen.

White countertops and sunny yellow cabinets help to brighten a kitchen without a lot of natural light.

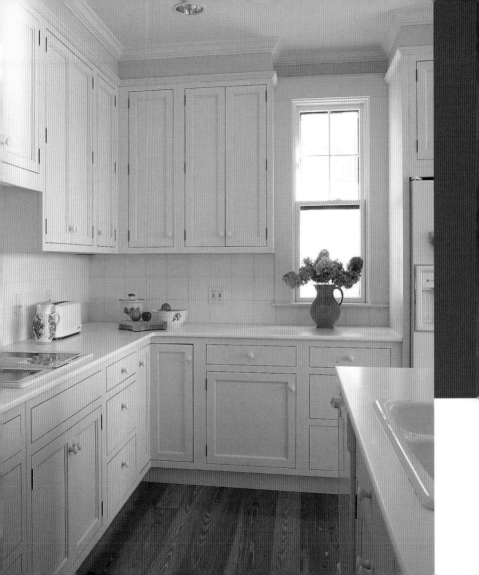

If you don't have a lot of money but want to give your kitchen a new look, paint the cabinets and change the hardware.

cabinets

Glass doors on both sides of this
ceiling-hung cabinet help to keep an
open feeling between the kitchen and
the adjacent eating area.

Painting dingy
cabinets
instantly
freshens up
the kitchen.

Before painting
kitchen cabinets,
remove all hinges, knobs,
and shelves, then
scrub everything
with painters' detergent
to clean off dirt and grease.

Above Sturdy drop-down doors flank this high-powered range to provide heat-proof work surfaces when they're open and hideaway storage compartments when they're not.

Right What might have been empty wall space below upper cabinets was turned into unique supply shelves.

Bright red and yellow steel cabinets accompany a stainless-steel backsplash and retro-looking hardware to create a 1950s flavor.

Any vent hood should pipe the exhaust outdoors. Blowing it back into the room offers little benefit, other than to help dry a freshly showered chef's hair.

Open cabinets
allow you to
display pretty objects
like pottery and baskets of
fresh fruits and
vegetables—plus
they cost a lot less
than those with drawers
and doors.

Painting these dated
cabinets green and adding
natural wood knobs gave
the kitchen a pleasing new
identity with only a few
days of work.

Open-air shelving keeps supplies at hand and helps to make a compact space feel larger.

A cookbook shelf should be 8 in. deep, one for dishware should be about 15 in. deep, and one for pans and appliances should be at least 18 in. deep.

The easy-to-clean surfaces of laminate cabinets meld well with minimalist contemporary decorating.

Make over your laminate cabinets with paint that's specially formulated for sticking to their slick surfaces.

The type and style of cabinets will define the look and feel of a kitchen.

Eight beat-up drawers salvaged from an old stationery store were repaired, given new pulls, and installed with heavy-duty drawer glides in a bank of custom cabinets.

If you have kids,

consider turning your

wine cooler into

a snack station

so small tikes can

reach with ease.

This wet bar is positioned so that it's
not in the way of traffic flow. The color
makes it a focal point as well.

With the cabinet door
around the corner, a
slight recess in this end
panel provides a spot
for keeping hand towels
within easy reach but out
of the way.

Punched-tin panels take the place of wood or glass in these country-style cabinets.

With cabinets and windows competing for limited wall space, a
wall unit was installed right over a picture window.

When renovating,
focus your resources on
the "bones" of the kitchen,
such as cabinets, flooring,
and fixtures.
You can always replace the
appliances and countertops later.

Opaque glass, such as these sand-blasted panes, provides an open look while keeping messy and overstuffed shelves obscured.

Inlayed wood trim can give even simple cabinets a distinctive look.

Wood panels can help to blend appliances with the cabinets for a sophisticated traditional look in the kitchen.

New knobs and pulls
can add instant
style to cabinet doors
and drawers.

Flipper doors at the end of a breakfast bar open to reveal a compact message center for keeping track of mail and other important items—and a television on a swiveling slide-out drawer.

Pull-out baskets make casual drawers for storing root vegetables that benefit from getting plenty of fresh air or oversized tools.

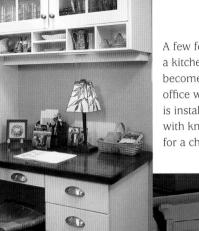

A few feet of wall space in a kitchen or dining area can become a functional home office when a countertop is installed at desk height with knee space underneath for a chair.

Create a
mini
mudroom
by the back
door by
outfitting a
pantry cabinet
with
cubbies
and
coat hooks.

countertops
& sinks

Earth tones set the stage in this kitchen, with visual interest coming from the tile backsplash and granite countertop.

Multiple countertops materials—solid surfacing for the work areas, decorative tile for a raised bar, and stone for the center island—add visual appeal to a large, neutral-colored kitchen.

·····································

Keep ceramic tile
countertops looking great
over the long term by
installing them with
stain-resistant epoxy grout.

·····································

The rounded lip on these countertops makes them look like stone or solid surfacing, but they're actually made from economical laminate.

Walls and countertops covered with Japanese raku tiles have an iridescent crackled surface.

A low countertop (right) is the ideal spot for baking projects, which tend to require a lot of elbow grease. Just move the bouquet (below) and this stone slab is ready for kneading dough or setting up a stand mixer, thanks to the outlet in the backsplash.

Turn the dishwashing soaps on your counter into decorating assets by decanting them into antique glass bottles with pour spouts.

Soapstone sinks and countertops are authentic 19th-century details.

Keep kitchen germs at bay by handling products on dishwasher-safe plastic

meat and dairy
cutting boards.

Above An inset pastry marble and cutting board create efficient work surfaces on a tiled countertop.

Left A heat-proof soapstone insert in this wood-topped island provides a convenient spot for setting down hot pans taken out of oven.

The key square pattern in the floor is repeated half-size on the backsplash, lending a sense of scale to the space.

Natural mineral deposits on honed slate make this backsplash an eye-catching focal point.

Granite is the gold standard for countertops since it's undamaged by knives, spills, or hot pans.

Granite tiles with color-matched grout create the look of slab-stone countertops for less than half the cost.

Add drama
to your kitchen by
contrasting the colors
of the countertop
and cabinets.
Use hardware to pull
the look together.

Faucets and pot fillers come in a variety of styles and materials. Many come with an option of a matching sprayer and soap dispenser.

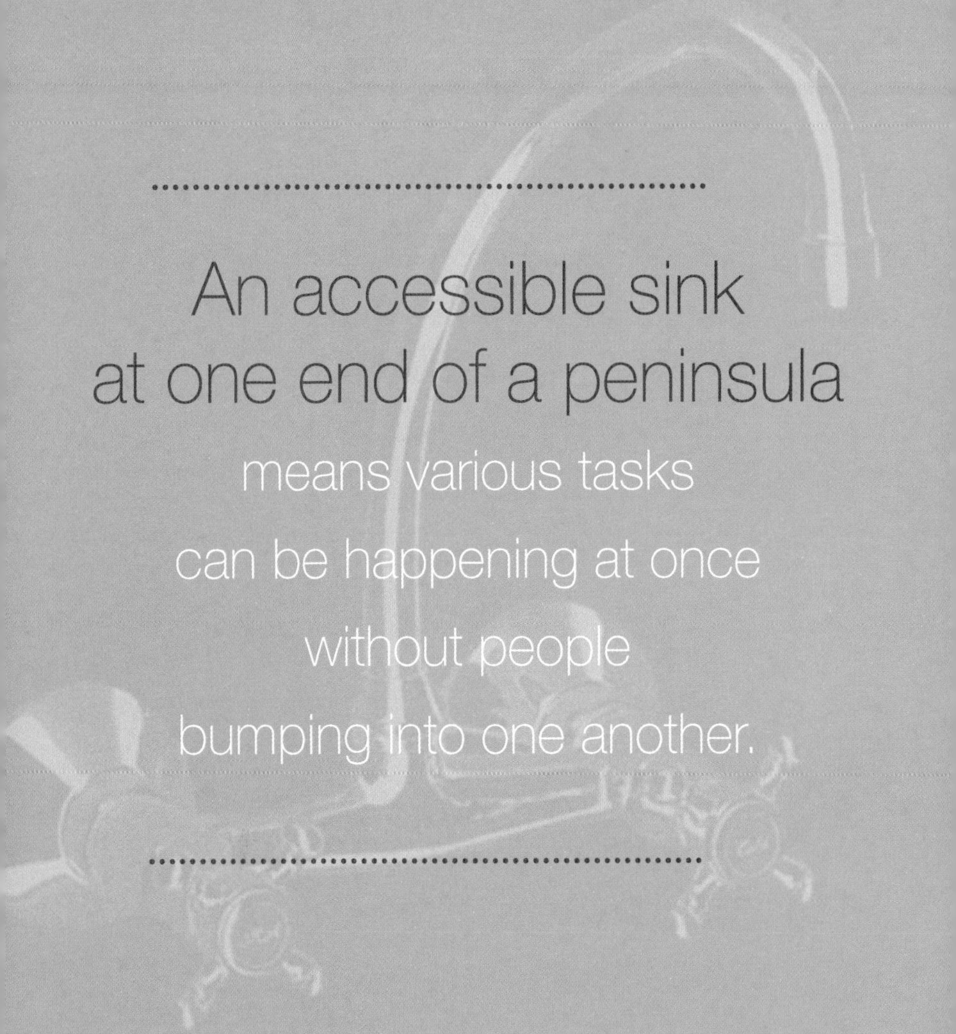

An accessible sink
at one end of a peninsula
means various tasks
can be happening at once
without people
bumping into one another.

Vegetable trimmings can be scraped into
a garbage pail—or compost bucket—
through an access door in the countertop.

An extra deep sink reduces splashing,
eliminating the need for a backsplash,
and allowing the sink to share space
with a breakfast bar.

Incorporating decorative tiles into a backsplash provides a
big bang for your buck because you only need a few.

Kitchen counters must be easy to work on and to clean, but they also add to the look of the kitchen. Consider granite, concrete, acrylic, classic butcher block, tile, or stainless steel.

A Portuguese tile mosaic above the cooktop injects color and drama into an otherwise white-on-white kitchen.

appliances

Make a message center
of the refrigerator by
incorporating a
chalkboard door.

Double-drawer dishwashers conserve energy because you can run one drawer at a time.

Create a calmer kitchen
at cleanup time

by choosing one of the ultra-quiet

dishwashers available today.

Every now and then, dump out your ice cube basket, because over time the cubes absorb freezer odors.

Left Built-in refrigerator and freezer drawers provide easy access to foodstuffs right where you need them—a particular advantage to people with mobility problems.

Right The biggest advantage to side-by-side refrigerators is their in-door ice and water dispensers.

Locating a wall oven and cooktop together gives them the unusual look of a built-in one-piece range.

Play it safe by
upgrading all kitchen outlets to modern GFCIs, which are designed to prevent shocks.

An aluminum door lifts up to expose a garage full of appliances—and conveniently located electrical outlets.

Look for nuggets of space to store anything from foodstuffs to dishware. Just be sure you want to look at whatever you're leaving out in the open.

A microwave can take up precious counter space, so if possible, put it on a shelf (above) or hang it underneath a cabinet. When it does sit on the counter, make sure there's plenty of space around it for setting hot dishes (right).

··

There's no need to replace
all of your appliances
at the same time.

If the budget is tight, upgrade your

appliances one at a time

as finances allow.

··

Since everyone opens the refrigerator more often
than the freezer, some appliances put the fridge on
top, meaning you won't have to bend down to seek
out that jar of lemonade or slice of leftover pizza.

Install professional-style appliances to get higher-grade safety features

—instead of true restaurant equipment—
such as insulated oven doors.

One of the biggest ad-
vantages of a separate
cooktop is that you can
store pots and pans in
drawers or on shelves
right below it.

There's nothing beautiful about a microwave, so hide it in a cabinet with a flip-up door for easy access.

Dishwashers belong on the left of the sink for right-handed chefs and to the right of the sink for lefties.

A glass-smooth
cooktop with
a downdraft vent
practically disappears into
the black countertop
around it.

eating areas

A full-sized kitchen table makes the formal dining room unnecessary, so you can convert that space to another use, such as a family room or home office.

A drop-leaf table is a great way to put a small space to good use. When in service, more guests can be accommodated.

Left alone, this antique pedestal table acts as a simple cooking island, but bring in a few dining room chairs and it becomes a comfortable spot for a casual family meal.

As trendy as islands are, a simple kitchen table can be just as useful—especially in a traditional kitchen. With a top that matches the countertops, it feels like a permanent part of the kitchen.

An overhanging countertop and a few pull-up stools are all you need to create a breakfast buffet in any kitchen.

Create just the right mood in your eat-in kitchen by installing dimmer switches for the light fixtures.

A restaurant-style booth requires only half the floor space of a standard table and chair set, and it's a lot cozier, too.

Save money on kitchen stools by buying them from an online specialty shop.

If your island or peninsula allows, put seating on multiple sides so that diners can see each other and converse more easily than if they were sitting in a line.

Each distinct area of this open-floor-plan room adds its own touch of color, including the chairs at the eating counter.

An antique bench stands ready to provide extra seating for guests—though it's the table that must be moved toward the heavy bench.

Installing an eating surface 30 in. off the ground means you can use standard chairs—and that the buffet will be wheelchair accessible.

This empty corner has become a cozy eating nook, thanks to store-bought cushioned benches and a standard kitchenette set.

storage &
organization

Sliding lids onto their pot handles
before you hang the pots ensures that
you'll never again have to go searching
for the right top—and eliminates the
mess of lid storage.

A narrow shelf built high along the beadboard backsplash turns unused space into storage for everything from spices to jars of baby food.

If your older kitchen
has a built-in
ironing board
that doesn't get used,
remove it, install some
shelves, and you've got
a large in-wall
spice rack.

Above Adjustable drawer dividers can be custom-fit to whatever you are storing.

Right A pull-out broom closet makes use of a narrow space alongside wall ovens.

Opposite Wire shelves are an inexpensive way to add storage to a busy kitchen. Install one right over the range and it'll even keep food warm until serving time.

Snap-top glass canisters keep ingredients fresh, make it easy to see when you need to replenish supplies, and proudly display the beauty of foods.

Uniform jars and labels make it easy to alphabetize spices and to keep them organized.

Locate all tools for a particular task together to create an efficient work area.

A slot in a wood countertop makes for safe, easy-access knife storage.

A bank of cabinets surrounding a wall oven keeps bakeware close to the action.

Older homes
come with storage
challenges.
Use modular metal
shelving around a
freestanding
stove to provide storage

A narrow shelf with plexiglass guard rails turns the inside of a closet door into a well-stocked spice rack.

For a chef who cooks a wide range of international dishes, a small spice rack wouldn't do. A large wall shelf has become a trophy case for interesting ingredients and condiments collected around the world.

Here's an space-saving way to store spices: Pack them into steel canisters and arrange them on magnetic strips fastened to the side of a cabinet wall.

Herbs and spices
lose their
potency after 1 to 3
years on the shelf,
so mark the date on
new purchases and you'll know
when to replace aging supplies.

Look high and low for space equipment and serving dishes.

The high cabinet above the refrigerator calls for storing a rarely used pot and wines that need some time to age. It also calls for keeping a kitchen stool handy.

Deep drawers with heavy-duty glides provide an out-of-the-way spot for stashing pots and pans with their lids in place.

Incorporate flexible spaces that work for you. Rolling carts function well for both storage and additional work surface; shelves that slide out enable you to access hard-to-reach items.

Pullout shelves (left) make it easy to reach everything that's stashed in a deep cabinet—even the stuff in the back. For corner cabinets (right), lazy Susans are essential for accessing every ounce of storage space.

Many types of pull-out accessories make getting at the trash and recycling cans easy. Look for wood and plastic-coated wire types that can be retrofitted into existing cabinets.

Garbage and recycling cans are hidden in this slant-top unit made to look like the bulk storage bins from old-fashioned general stores.

Create a place
to stow recyclables
right in your kitchen
and setting them aside
won't be such a chore.

·······················

If your style is traditional,
look for an old butcher
block at flea markets;
clean it up and use it
as a place to chop vegetables as
well as a decorative accent.

·······················

This homemade rolling island is multi-purpose, making it as useful as a chopping surface as it is as a movable serving surface.

A pull-out shelf can turn the clutter of your under-the-sink cabinet into an organized and easy-to-reach supply depot.

A shallow back-of-the-door caddy provides an ideal spot for storing sink and dishwasher supplies.

This simple cabinet accessory keeps a trash can accessible and out of sight.

Rather than hogging countertop space, this dish drainer hangs over
the sink.

if you use materials
decorating scheme.

Keep towels at the ready by hanging them where they can reached at a moment's notice.

A knife-drawer insert keeps blades sharp, well organized, and out of reach of youngsters' fingers.

··

That sharpening "steel"
in your knife block will keep an
edge on a sharp knife
but won't sharpen a dull one.
Bring dull knives to a local kitchen supply
or hardware store for a true sharpening.

··

Pop-up mixer shelves lock into place at a convenient work height until it's time to stow away the heavy and bulky stand mixer, when the entire shelf and mixer lower effortlessly into a dedicated cabinet.

Hanging racks for kitchen tools can be simple and ordinary or become a design element itself. Whatever you choose, ensure the most-used items are kept close at hand.

Want a pantry but don't think you have the room? Think again.

Tap into unused space between the wall studs.

Create a pantry in a base-ment stairwell by adding shallow shelves to the wall.

The unique drawers on each side of this sink (top) offer more room than the typical flip-down drawer. A plastic container with snap-tight lid was retrofitted in this drawer (bottom) for compost scraps; the container can be removed for easy use.

....

Keep drawers organized

by designating each one

for tools or supplies

used for a specific task.

....

A simple grid of cubbies in a base cabinet holds a dozen bottles of wine on their sides, ensuring that the corks stay moist, which is essential for preventing spoilage.

Store wine in a
cool, dry place,
particularly bottles
you want to hold
onto until
the wine has aged.

Kitchen storage goes beyond cooking tools and dishware. Keep essential supplies in a designated drawer with dividers to keep everything organized (left). Retrofit a door face to flip down to expose a laptop computer (top).

floors

Large floor tiles make a space seem more expansive, especially when the grout is the same color as the tile.

Textured vinyl tile flooring can look a lot like slate for a fraction of the cost.

Hardwood exudes warmth and sophistication but can blend in with cabinetry if both are part of the same color family. Small rugs add color and can help to define spaces.

A red linoleum floor gives this all-white kitchen energy and combines well with the cabinets and appliances to create a retro look.

Setting a checkerboard floor on the diagonal lends charm to the room and can make it feel bigger, too.

Give an old wood floor an instant facelift by painting it with a colorful tile-like design.

Cork flooring looks like a cross between solid wood and speckled linoleum, but it's made from bark and is filled with millions of tiny air cells that make it comfortable under foot.

Be kind to
your aching feet:
Wear
cushioned slippers,
stand on a carpet,
or sit on a stool
during marathon cooking
projects.

Get wood
floors without the
mess of
sanding and sealing
by installing prefinished
flooring, which has a super-
tough factory finish.

A hardwood floor is great if you have kids and pets who tend to track in a mess, since the color hides dirt and the floor itself is easy to clean quickly.

details &
accessories

Any large ceramic
planter can be used
for cooking utensils.

Add task lighting anywhere you need it with battery-powered LED disks

that have adhesive backings.

Under-cabinet lights illuminate countertops without making the overall room too bright.

Busy checkerboard tile countertops and backsplashes call for a simple window treatment, which is provided by a 10-in. gathered valance in a mini-check print.

When choosing tiles, keep in mind that darker colors absorb light so work well where there's plenty of light. Backsplashes and cooking alcoves are ideal spots for light-colored tiles.

A natural woven wood shade doesn't block out the sun entirely, but it reduces glare while allowing dappled light into the room.

The strong horizontal texture of these woven wood shades counterbalances the vertical lines of the wall paneling and also picks up the natural veining in the marble countertops.

Set high enough to protect privacy, transom windows are left without shades so that natural light flows into the house even when the shades below are drawn.

Sheer linen Roman shades works together to smarten a row of kitchen windows and can be lowered individually as the sunlight shifts across the horizon.

A speckled carpet in front of the sink offers a gentle landing for weary feet—and a playful harmony with the stippled granite countertops.

Add personality to your kitchen by displaying artwork, family photos, or knick-knacks. The wide brim of the hood prevents grease and cooking grime from tarnishing the figurines.

Herbs will thrive on a kitchen windowsill; plus, they add texture to the decorating scheme, fragrance to the air, and are just an arm's length away when they're needed for a favorite recipe.

A chalkboard can be a lifesaver

when family members are on the go. Locate it where everyone can see it.

Like the look of glass doors but don't want to have to keep the contents orderly? Install café curtains on the bottom half, exposing only the areas you want to display.

sources

organizations

American Institute
of Architects (AIA)
1735 New York Ave. NW
Washington, DC 200006
www.aiaaccess.com

American Society of
Interior Designers (ASID)
608 Massachusetts Ave. NE
Washington, DC 20002
www.interiors.org

National Association of
Home Builders (NAHB)
1201 Fifteenth St. NW
Washington, DC 20005
www.nahb.org

National Association of
Professional Organizers
www.napo.net

National Association of the
Remodeling Industry (NARI)
4900 Seminary Road #3210
Alexandria, VA 22311
www.nari.org

National Kitchen & Bath
Association
687 Willow Grove St.
Hackettstown, NJ 07840
www.nkba.com

web sites

Decorating Den Interiors
www.decoratingden.com

Dr. Toy
www.drtoy.com

Energy Star
www.energystar.com/gov

Get Decorating
www.GetDecorating.com

HomePortfolio
www.homeportfolio.com

The Building and Home
Improvement Directory
www.build.com

U.S. Consumer Product
Safety Commission
www.cpsc.gov

product sources

Alkco® Lighting
www.alkco.com

American Standard®
www.americanstandard.com

Babybox.com
www.babybox.com

Bed, Bath & Beyond®
www.bedbathandbeyond.com

Bernhardt Furniture
Company
www.bernhardt.com

Blanco®
www.blancoamerica.com

Broadway Panhandler
www.broadwaypanhandler.com

Broyhill Furniture
Industries, Inc.
www.broyhillfurn.com

California Closets®
www.californiaclosets.com

Casabella®
www.casabella.com

CD Storehouse
(800) 829-4203

Chicago Faucets®
www.chicagofaucets.com

Closet Factory
www.closetfactory.com

ClosetMaid®
www.closetmaid.com

The Conran Shop
www.conran.com

The Container Store
www.containerstore.com

Corian®
www.corian.com

Crate & Barrel
www.crateandbarrel.com

Country Floors®
www.countryfloors.com

Dacor®
www.dacor.com

Design Within Reach
www.dwr.com

Elkay®
www.elkayusa.com

Exposures®
www.exposuresonline.com

Filofax®
www.filofax.com

Franke® Sinks & Faucets
www.frankeksd.com

Freedom Bag®
www.freedombag.com

Frigidaire®
www.frigidaire.com

Frontgate®
www.frontgate.com

General Electric®
www.geappliances.com

Graber Window Fashions
www.springs.com

Gracious Home
www.gracioushome.com

Harden Furniture, Inc.
www.harden.com

Halo® Lighting
www.cooperlighting.com

Hold Everything®
www.holdeverything.com

HomeDecInASec
www.homedecinasec.com

Ikea®
www.ikea.com

Jenn-Air®
www.jennair.com

KitchenAid®
www.kitchenaid.com

Kmart™
www.kmart.com

Knape & Vogt
www.knapeandvogt.com

Kohler® Plumbing
www.us.kohler.com

Kraftmaid®
www.kraftmaid.com

The Land of Nod
www.thelandofnod.com

Lamps Plus
www.lampsplus.com

Lane Home Furnishings
www.lanefurniture.com

Levenger®
www.levenger.com

Lightolier®
www.lightolier.com

Mannington, Inc.
www.mannington.com

Maytag®
www.maytag.com

Moen®
www.moen.com

Netkidswear.com
www.netkidswear.com

Poliform
www.poliformusa.com

Posh Tots
www.poshtots.com

Rejuvenation lighting
and hardware
www.rejuvenation.com

Restoration Hardware℠
www.restorationhardware.com

Rev-A-Shelf
www.rev-a-shelf.com

Rubbermaid®
www.rubbermaid.com

Seabrook Wallcoverings
www.seabrookwallcoverings.com

Serena & Lily
www.serenaandlily.com

Stacks and Stacks
www.stacksandstacks.com

Target®
www.target.com

Thermador®
www.thermador.com

Thomasville Furniture
Industries
www.thomasville.com

Tupperware®
www.tupperware.com

Umbra®
www.umbra.com

Velux America, Inc.
www.veluxusa.com

Vermont Soapstone
Company
www.vermontsoapstone.com

Viking®
www.vikingrange.com

WallCandy Arts
www.wallcandyarts.com

Wallies
www.wallies.com

The Warm Biscuit Bedding
Company
www.warmbiscuit.com

Wicanders® Cork Flooring
www.wicanders.com

Wolf®
www.subzero.com/wolf

York Wallcoverings
www.yorkwall.com

photo credits

pp. ii-iii: Photo: © Ken Gutmaker.

p. v: (left) Photo: © Kate Roth; (middle) Photo: © Jason McConathy; (right) Photo: © Rob Karosis.

p. vi: (far left) Photo: © www.davidduncanlivingston.com; (left) Photo: © Rob Karosis; (middle) Photo: © Ken Gutmaker; (right) Photo: © 2006 Carolyn L. Bates, www.carolynlbates.com.

p. 1: (far left) Photo: © Rob Karosis; (left) Photo: © 2006 Carolyn L. Bates, www.carolynlbates.com; (middle) Photo: © The Taunton Press, Inc.; (right) Photo: © Ken Gutmaker

CHAPTER 1

p. 3: Photo: © www.davidduncanlivingston.com.

p. 4: Photo: © Rob Karosis.

p. 6: Photo: © Eric Roth.

p. 7: Photo: © 2006 Carolyn L. Bates, www.carolynlbates.com.

p. 9: Photo: © Rob Karosis.

p. 10: Photo: © Grey Crawford

p. 12: Photo: © Jason McConathy.

p. 13: Photo: © www.davidduncanlivingston.com.

p. 14: Photo: © Ken Gutmaker.

p. 16: Photo: © Bill Ruth, Design: Rob Hetler Cabinetmaker.

p. 17: Photo: © 2006 Carolyn L. Bates, www.carolynlbates.com.

pp. 18–19: Photo: © Brian Vanden Brink.

p. 20: Photo: © Rob Karosis.

p. 21: Photo: © Eric Roth.

pp. 22–23: Photo: © Ken Gutmaker.

p. 24: Photo: © www.davidduncanlivingston.com.

p. 25: Photo: © 2006 Carolyn L. Bates, www.carolynlbates.com.

p. 26–27: Photo: Scott Gibson, © The Taunton Press, Inc., Cabinetmaker: Serge Therrien.

CHAPTER 2

p. 29: Photo: © Rob Karosis.

p. 30: Photo: courtesy the Kennebec Company.

p. 32: (top) Photo: © Brian Vanden Brink, Design: Jane Langmuir Interior Design.

p. 33: Photo: © Rob Karosis.

p. 34: Photo: © Jason McConathy.

p. 37: Photo: © Ken Gutmaker.

pp. 38–39: Photo: © Rob Karosis.

p. 40: Photo: Charles Bickford, © The Taunton Press, Inc.

p. 41: Photo: © 2006 Carolyn L. Bates, www.carolynlbates.com.

p. 42: Photo: © Ken Gutmaker.

p. 45: Photo: © Susan Kahn.

p. 46: Photo: © David Ericson, Design: Patrick W. McClane.

p. 48: Photo: © www.davidduncanlivingston.com.

p. 49: Photo: Scott Gibson, © The Taunton Press, Inc.

p. 50: Photo: © Rob Karosis.

p. 52: Photo: © The Taunton Press, Inc., Cabinetmaker: Thompson and Brouillette, Inc.

p. 53: Photo: © 2006 Carolyn L. Bates, www.carolynlbates.com.

p. 54: Photo: © John Rapetti/Carol Kurth Associates.

p. 56: (left) Photo: courtesy Liberty Hardware Manufacturing; (right) Photo: © Charles Wilkins.

p. 57: (top left) Photo: Karen Tanaka, © The Taunton Press, Inc.; (top right) Photo: © Ken Gutmaker; (bottom) Photo: © H. Durston Saylor.

p. 128: Photo: © Rob Karosis.

p. 129: Photo: © 2006 Carolyn L. Bates, www.carolynlbates.com.

CHAPTER 6

p. 131: Photo: © 2006 Carolyn L. Bates, www.carolynlbates.com.

p. 132: Photo: © Ken Gutmaker.

p. 134: (top) Photo: Karen Tanaka, © The Taunton Press, Inc.; (bottom) Photo: © Kate Roth.

p. 134: Photo: © Tim Street-Porter.

p. 136: (left) Photo: © Eric Piasecki; (right) Photo: © Amy Albert.

pp. 137–139: Photos: Karen Tanaka, © The Taunton Press, Inc.

p. 140: Photo: © Susan Kahn.

pp. 142–144: Photos: © Grey Crawford.

pp. 146–174: Photos: © Ken Gutmaker.

p. 148: (left and middle) Photos: © The Taunton Press, Inc., Design: Flo Braker.

p. 149: Photo: © Alloc, Inc., www.alloc.com.

p. 150: Photo: © www.davidduncanlivingston.com.

p. 151: Photo: Scott Gibson, © The Taunton Press, Inc.

p. 152: (top) Photo: Charles Miller, © The Taunton Press, Inc.; (bottom) Photo: © Robert Perron, Design: Strittmatter Kitchens and Baths.

p. 154: Photo: © Brian Vanden Brink, Design: Tom Hampson.

p. 157: Photo: © Aaron Pennock.

p. 158: Photo: © Knape and Vogt Architects.

p. 159: (left) Photo: courtesy Kraftmaid Cabinetry; (right) Photo: © Knape and Vogt Architects.

p. 160: Photo: © Grey Crawford.

p. 161: Photo: © Brian Vanden Brink.

p. 162: Photo: © Grey Crawford.

p. 164: Karen Tanaka, © The Taunton Press, Inc.

p. 165: Photo: © The Taunton Press, Inc., Design: Anne Otterson.

p. 166: Photo: © 2006 Carolyn L. Bates, www.carolynlbates.com.

p. 167: (top) Photo: Charles Miller, © The Taunton Press, Inc.; (bottom) Photo: © 2006 Carolyn L. Bates, www.carolynlbates.com.

p. 169: Photo:© Jason McConathy.

p. 170: (top) Photo: © Brian Vanden Brink; (bottom) Photo: © John Marckworth.

pp. 172–173: Photo: © www.davidduncanlivingston.com.

p. 174: Photo: Charles Miller, © The Taunton Press, Inc.

p. 175: Photo: © Rob Karosis.

CHAPTER 7

p. 177: Photo: © The Taunton Press, Inc.

p. 178: Design: Thunder Mill Design.

p. 179: Photo: © Brian Vanden Brink, Design: 10 Oakes Interiors.

pp. 180–181: Photo: © Gail Owens.

p. 183: Photo: © 2006 Carolyn L. Bates, www.carolynlbates.com.

pp. 184–185: Photo: © Brian Vanden Brink.

p. 187: Photo: © Brian Vanden Brink.

CHAPTER 8

p. 189: Photo: © Ken Gutmaker.

p. 190: Photo: © Randy O'Rourke.

p. 191: Photo: © Ken Gutmaker.

p. 192: Photo: © 2006 Carolyn L. Bates, www.carolynlbates.com.